Re:CONSIDERING

THE PLEASURES OF PESSIMISM

Natasha Moore

Published by Acorn Press, an imprint of Bible Society Australia, in partnership with the Centre for Public Christianity.
ACN 127 775 973
GPO Box 4161
Sydney NSW 2001
Australia

www.publicchristianity.org

ISBN 978-0-647-53075-7 (pbk)
ISBN 978-0-647-53076-4 (ebk)

A catalogue record for this book is available from the National Library of Australia

Editor: Kristin Argall
Cover and text design: John Healy
Cover illustration: Nell Healy

About the Centre for Public Christianity

What is the good life?
What does it mean to be human?
Where can I find meaning?
Who can I trust?

In sceptical and polarised times, the Centre for Public Christianity (CPX) seeks to engage the public with a clear, balanced, and surprising picture of the Christian faith. A not-for-profit media company, since 2007 CPX has been joining the dots between contemporary culture and the enduring story of Jesus in the articles, podcasts, books, documentaries, and other resources we produce.

We believe Christianity still has something vital to say about life's biggest questions. Find out more about our team and the work we do at www.publicchristianity.org or follow us on Facebook, Twitter, and Instagram.

About the author

Natasha Moore is a Research Fellow at the Centre for Public Christianity in Sydney. She has a PhD in English Literature from the University of Cambridge and is the author of *Victorian Poetry and Modern Life: The Unpoetical Age* and *For the Love of God: How the church is better and worse than you ever imagined.* She recently discovered she is an optimist.

CONTENTS

This material began life as the 2019 ADM Annual Lecture 'The Pleasures of Pessimism: On hope, culture, and the end of the world'. My thanks to ADM for getting me started down this apocalyptic road.

Re:CONSIDERING

INTRODUCTION: WELCOME TO THE APOCALYPSE

I think it was 2013 when it really, truly occurred to me that everything might get worse.

I mean, I knew theoretically that civilisations fall and ecosystems crash. I could wedge 'Orwellian' into a sentence as casually as the next person; I was consuming at least my fair share of post-apocalyptic stories on the big and small screen. I was spending most of my time competing for an ever-shrinking pool of jobs in the wake of what only Australians call the GFC. It was also the year I turned 30, so, you know.

Then I stumbled, in quick succession, on a series of reports that abruptly closed the distance, for me, between theoretical and *oh you mean this reality, the one I'm in*.

There was the warning from the US Centers for Disease Control and Prevention that humanity was on the cusp of 'a post-antibiotic era'. As drug-resistant superbugs proliferated, we could be facing a world where a minor cut might once again kill you. Organ transplants and routine surgery would become too risky; more women would die in childbirth; many cancer treatments would be impossible. I had been naively thinking of progress, at least of the scientific-medical kind, as locked in. Not so.

There were also rumblings about the so-called 'supervolcano' lurking with intent under Yellowstone. The magma reservoir was turning out to be way bigger than we thought, and geologists argued about whether an explosion that would blanket most of the continental US and plunge the globe into a volcanic winter might be imminent.

And then there was the jellification of the oceans.

I was startled to read that jellyfish have at times shut down nuclear power plants, caused a blackout that was mistaken for the beginnings of a political coup, capsized a trawler, and even vanquished a US aircraft carrier. One species single-handedly destroyed the Black Sea fishing industry, on which three national economies depended.

As other marine species struggle to survive in increasingly acidic and oxygen-depleted oceans, jellyfish thrive – and speed both the extinction of their competitors and potentially even climate change itself. Jellyfish blooms can form a kind of 'curtain of death' such as the one covering more than 30,000 square miles off southern Africa, I read. Ere long, they may be the last species standing – floating – in our oceans. Swell.

No article you read about the looming jellyfish apocalypse neglects to mention the Irukandji. Found off the northern coasts of Australia – and increasingly elsewhere in the world as well – the Irukandji is one of the deadliest creatures in a country not lacking in creatures that can kill you. Its bigger cousin, the box jellyfish, will kill you quicker, in under four minutes; Irukandjis take longer, and death is not guaranteed.

But I think they compel such horrified fascination because they're close to invisible (colourless, with a bell that might be no larger than a peanut); the sting itself is so minor as to be barely noticeable; and the symptoms of 'Irukandji syndrome', which begin perhaps a half hour later, are so extreme. It starts with back pain and moves through a feeling of crawling skin, agitation, and vomiting every minute or so for the next twelve hours, to possible cardiac arrest, respiratory failure, or brain haemorrhage.

And no description of an Irukandji sting fails to mention a further symptom: a sense of 'impending doom'. Victims beg doctors to kill them – to escape the pain, but also the existential dread that accompanies it.

I'm not sure why it was these stories in particular that cut through my complacency, my unconscious assumption that things would trundle on more or less as they were in my relatively charmed little historical and geopolitical pocket. But I write this in the summer of 2020, in a city blanketed in smoke, with 'fires near me' topping Australians' list of Google search terms and #WorldWar3 trending on Twitter. It's going to print in the middle of the worst global pandemic for a century. Which is really to say that, of late, the Irukandji has taken on for me the force of a parable.

There are things going wrong in our world. Things that maybe didn't seem so bad at the time – things we might not even have noticed at the time – suddenly escalate alarmingly, perhaps mysteriously. We don't always know what stung us. We don't know if we'll survive.

But distinct from and binding together all the disparate symptoms is a generalised despair: as reported by sufferers across the board, an overwhelming sense of doom.

Cassandra vs Chicken Little

It is characteristic of our cultural moment that, while everyone will readily concede that things are going wrong, nobody agrees on which things, or how wrong.

Progressives and conservatives, religious believers and secularists, boomers and millennials project mutually incompatible apocalypses. We disagree on who's to blame and what to do about it. We disagree on whether our forebears had it better or worse, and whether they were tougher than us.

Of course, most of the time now, what we talk about when we talk about the end of the world is climate change. And for obvious reasons. While far from being undisputed territory in our culture wars, if the warnings of the scientific community in this area represented the sole or even main focus of our forebodings about the future, that would make us simply prudent, not pessimistic.

But our declinism – our instinct that everything is going off the rails, or is just about to – is far, far more generalised. For the connoisseur of catastrophe, the news offers a ghoulish smorgasbord of options.

Climate projections are a staple, yes; but the old meat-and-three-veg option of nuclear holocaust, while looking a little stodgy by comparison, makes a periodic comeback. For those with more adventurous tastes, there's our coming robot overlords, or the potentially dystopian implications of transhumanism of one variety or another. Anyone who savours speculation about that Yellowstone supervolcano can consume a steady diet of other looming natural disaster stories – such as the earthquake-plus-tsunami dubbed 'the really big one' due to decimate the Pacific Northwest of America over a period of 10 to 30 minutes sometime in the next perhaps 50 years.

And the menu of apocalyptic snacks and side dishes is endless:

IQ rates are falling in developed countries.

Our indoor, sedentary lifestyle is killing us.

Weapons of Math Destruction – big data – are increasing inequality and destroying democracy.

Cancel culture is coming for all of us.

Millennials bring their mums to job interviews.

Smartphones may have destroyed a generation.

Tinder is the dating apocalypse.

And here's one that's really stayed with me over the last few months, courtesy of CNN. The headline reads 'Cockroaches are becoming immune to insecticides. Have a great day', and the article begins:

> If it's not the heat death of the Earth that consumes us; if we are not snuffed out by blight, famine and the volatile hubris of mankind, it's only a matter of time before the cockroaches rise up and conquer us all. They are growing stronger.

Whether it's reduced funding for the arts or education or medical research, Gen Z's moral standards, political gridlock, political correctness gone mad, Ebola, or what happens when Amazon (or Google, or Disney+) controls every aspect of our lives, just about anything these days can be served up with a strong flavour of Armageddon.

Some of these threats are, of course, much more credible than others, and much more serious. But one effect of this constant background noise is to flatten out the distinctions and make it increasingly difficult to assess risk and respond to it sanely. Our general optimism or pessimism about the future has significant implications for how (and whether) we can muster the collective will to tackle the genuine crises that we face.

We have stories about this, templates to help us frame our sense of crisis.

One is the story of Cassandra. The god Apollo gave the Trojan princess the gift of seeing the future, but when she refused his amorous advances, he also set on her a curse: that though she would speak the truth, nobody would ever believe her prophecies. She warned her countrymen that Paris would fall in love with Helen and abduct her, sparking the Trojan War; that the city would be destroyed; that the Trojan horse was a ploy, that Greek warriors were hiding inside it; she even foresaw her own death. Yet she was consistently ignored or mocked for her negativity.

Proverbially, a Cassandra is doomed to be dismissed as hysterical, only to be vindicated – too late – as what they warned the rest of us about comes to pass.

Alternatively, there's Chicken Little. The folk tale comes in many versions, but the basic idea is: an acorn falls on Chicken Little's head, leading her to conclude that 'The sky is falling!' She sets out to inform the king that the end of the world is nigh, along the way convincing other easily excitable fowl – Ducky Lucky, Turkey Lurkey, Goosey Loosey – to join her in the quest. Before they get there, Foxy Loxy invites them to his lair and eats them all. (Chicken Little may or may not escape.)

The moral of the story? Don't panic – the sky

probably isn't falling, and while you're freaking out about that, something actually bad might happen to you. (In some versions, confusingly, the moral of the story is to have the courage of your convictions and to speak up.)

Optimists don't fare much better in our cultural mythology. To be 'Pollyanna-ish' – always cheerfully insisting that the glass is in fact brimming over – is not a compliment. Professor Pangloss, tutor to the young man Candide in Voltaire's novel of that name, caricatures one strand of the philosophical thought of his day, teaching his pupils that 'all is for the best' in this 'best of all possible worlds' – an optimism that the disaster-strewn narrative takes pains to expose as not just naïve but cruel.

So how do we know which one is us? Are we clear-eyed prophetesses, speaking truth to power only to meet hostility or inertia? Are we catastrophisers, prone to counterproductive panic over every bump in the road? Do we whistle in the dark, hoping our problems will go away, carefully managing our own mental state rather than tackling systemic ills? All of the above, perhaps, on one issue or another?

This little book does not try to adjudicate on the many arguments we are having as a culture about our collective future. It's not a book about the climate crisis – not because I doubt what scientists have long been telling us about anthropogenic climate change, or am blithe about what's required to address it anything like adequately. Rather, it's that I've been noticing some things about our public conversation, and the pessimism that pervades it, that I suspect make it much more difficult for us to take effective action on just about any issue you could name, including the hydra-headed challenges of a shifting climate. And I think we should talk about that.

Thus, this brief dispatch from a particular moment in the long history of human hopes and fears about the future; a moment of truce to ask questions like:

> Where does our declinism come from?
>
> What's so appealing about Armageddon? So pleasurable about pessimism?
>
> What might be helpful in it – and under what circumstances does it become definitely unhelpful?
>
> And what does all this say about our underlying, common (or uncommon) picture of reality?

Like everyone, I bring my own intellectual commitments and emotional leanings to this stuff. To put my cards on the table early, I count myself among the miscellaneous bunch broadly called Christians – as I expect will be obvious at certain points in what follows. My people have been thinking about the end of the world for millennia now (also about anxiety, suffering, justice, and other assorted concerns of relevance to the topic at hand), so this tradition is part of the gear I'm taking along as I wade into our increasingly jellyfish-laden cultural waters. It seems like we could use all the help we can get, frankly.

Woody Allen once wrote in *The New York Times*: 'More than at any time in history, mankind faces a crossroads. One path leads to despair and utter hopelessness. The other to total extinction. Let us pray we have the wisdom to choose correctly.' That was in 1979.

There are no easy solutions here, reader. I'm offering merely a chance to turn our gaze back on ourselves, and on what's going on for us as we fret about the future.

PART I: THE PLEASURES OF PESSIMISM

'If somebody's going to come, they'll come at night,' mutters Johnny O. He's wearing a ghillie suit as he commando crawls up to his own house, springing a surprise preparedness drill on his family.

'Doomsday preppers are very intelligent, out-of-the-box thinkers,' explains Johnny, who's concerned about the possibility of a terrorist attack on one of the four nuclear power plants situated not far from his Pennsylvania home. 'They're not average people. Sure, you may look at them and think that they're loony ... but you know what? Who are you going to turn to if something turns bad? You're going to go to the person that is prepared.'

Robert and Debbie Earl are more concerned about the collapse of the Greenland ice sheet, which they expect to happen much sooner than people think – leading to a cataclysmic rise in sea levels that could displace more than a billion people. They moved from Florida to the high desert hills of Alpine, Texas in order to get ready.

You might have seen an episode (or several) of National Geographic's *Doomsday Preppers*. It follows survivalists of various persuasions and evaluates their preparedness on a range of factors – food, water, shelter, security, and something called 'X factor' – in order to deliver a verdict: You have 12 months survival time. You have 10 months survival time.

You don't have to watch much *Doomsday Preppers* before it dawns on you that, however apprehensive its subjects claim to be about the end of the world as they know it, these people are also, surely, just a little bit ... *pumped*. Robert and Debbie, after being taught how to track and kill a deadly rattlesnake, toast the future over chunks of one of the desert's few abundant protein sources.

'Here's to further prepping,' Debbie proposes.

'And to doomsday!' chirps Robert.

We may like to think that dwelling on how everything is apparently getting worse is something we would rather *not* do. That, given the spike of fear and anxiety we get from stories of imminent decline or disaster, we would much prefer to be hearing good news about our collective future, if accurate (and possibly even if not).

This is dubious. Our clickbait habits, for starters, are against us here. I may not have much in common with the prepper movement – including my lack of any skills whatsoever that could prove useful in the event of civilisational collapse – but I'm willing to put my hand up and say: my name is Natasha, and I'm an apocaholic.

It's an addiction that takes a variety of forms. Newspaper editor Hugo Lindgren once wrote in *New York Magazine* about his own appetite for what he called 'pessimism porn.' His preferred flavour, he explains, is economic:

> The blog Calculated Risk is always a reliable turn-on. The guy who runs it combs the financial media for 'cliff-diving' rates of this and that. One data point he often cites is the A2P2 spread, or the difference 'between high- and low-quality 30-day nonfinancial commercial paper.' Turns out it 'gapped' dangerously last fall.
>
> Worrying about the A2P2 spread is like having a dirty secret. I spend many fruitful minutes playing out scenarios: What do I do when my corner deli gets looted? What bridge do I take out of town? There's something very exciting about it all.
>
> … Like real porn, the economic variety gives you the illusion of control, and similarly it only leaves you hungry for more. But econo-porn also feeds a powerful sense of intellectual vanity. You walk the streets feeling superior to all these heedless knaves who have no clue what's coming down the pike. By making yourself miserable about the frightful hell that awaits us, you feel better. Pessimism can be bliss too.

Studies of young people's expectations and hopes for the future have identified a similar sense of *enjoyed* trepidation. Without (one might argue) quite being clear on what it is they're wishing for, Australian youth, for example, have articulated sentiments such as these in interviews with sociologists:

> 'It's easy, for me anyway, to look at the world and think, God, let's prepare for the apocalypse. It's going to happen. I don't know if that's in part because of fear or hope. How much do I want the apocalypse to happen and just wipe this all clean?' (Elizabeth, 30)

> 'I would almost be disappointed if that wasn't how the world went in a weird way. I feel like that's a better way to go than to burn to the ground through hundreds and hundreds of terrible decisions.' (Isla, 27)

Before you throw this book across the room: I am perfectly willing to concede that you may not fit this bill. For those whose response to an uncertain and possibly catastrophic future is one of undiluted anxiety, or else despondency – those whose mental health has become a casualty of the relentless diet of bad news many of us consume – I have nothing but sympathy.

But for those who listen to Johnny, Robert and Debbie, Hugo, Elizabeth, or Isla and experience even a flicker of recognition … where does that come from? Why is pessimism so pleasurable?

I can think of at least three reasons.

It's in

'I know that it is thought essential to a man who has any knowledge of the world to have an extremely bad opinion of it', the philosopher John Stuart Mill remarked in a debate nearly 200 years ago. 'I have observed that not the man who hopes when others despair, but the man who despairs when others hope is admired by a large class of persons as a sage.'

This doesn't reflect us back to ourselves in a terribly flattering light, but at least part of pessimism's appeal comes down to its perennially fashionable status. The intellectual vanity Lindgren admits to is a powerful draw: *I* am in the know; *I* am bravely facing the grim realities of life. Unlike those schmucks over there.

Optimism is primary colours and American tourists in Europe and George Clooney as Batman and IKEA and lift music and Etsy. Pessimism is Reddit and bands nobody's heard of, and Christian Bale's Batman, and SBS and cold brew coffee.

Pessimism is the more sophisticated, worldly-wise cousin to optimism's country mouse. It is just edgier.

But deeper psychological waters await.

It's thrilling

At some level, the magnetic pull of destruction – our impulse to mentally rehearse the worst-case scenario – may be a self-preservation thing. Fictional versions of the apocalypse in particular can serve as a form of exposure therapy, allowing us to play out our fears in the safe space of prestige TV and disaster films. Ideally, we then return to our not-yet-completely-screwed reality with a new or renewed openness to the kind of change that might help prevent such a scenario.

It would be naïve, though, or else dishonest, to deny that the destruction itself holds a strange fascination for us.

This Freudian-sounding urge is not limited to disaster of the hypothetical kind. World War II historians note the uniformly apocalyptic terms in which that conflict has been described, both at the time and ever since. Only language evoking *the end of the world, hell, judgment day, cataclysm* has seemed adequate to the unprecedented implosion of the world in the 1930s and 1940s.

Keith Lowe, in his book *The Fear and the Freedom: Why the Second World War Still Matters*, argues that mingled with the horror and grief of those caught up in the destruction was something else: a 'wartime delight in annihilation – the more total, the more satisfying'.

This impulse, he suggests, was not limited to the 'bad guys'; it features in personal accounts from the 'heroes' and even victims of the war. We're familiar with the line uttered by nuclear physicist Robert Oppenheimer as he and his colleagues beheld the mushroom cloud produced by the first atom bomb test in July 1945: 'I am become death, the destroyer of worlds.' Later on, in interviews, Oppenheimer would always repeat these words – from the Hindu epic, the *Bhagavad Gita* – with a fitting solemnity. Contemporary accounts, though, suggest that first delivery was accompanied by a little bit of a strut: there was something intoxicating about the power and scale of the weapon.

But according to Lowe, it was not only those safe at home behind glass who experienced this kind of rush. He describes one inhabitant of Hamburg, for example – virtually levelled in the firestorm created by the 1943 bombing dubbed Operation

Gomorrah – who admitted to *willing the bombers on*, 'eager to see the total destruction of his city despite his simultaneous horror of it'.

There's something primal and not a little disturbing in this – in the *aesthetic* element to the apocalypse. If things are going to go bad, is there something in us that wants them to be *very* bad? Do we want the destruction to be, in Lowe's words, 'bigger, more beautiful, more total'?

If our world – whatever the scale of that world – must end, there's some part of the human psyche that would prefer it to end not with a whimper, but with the most dramatic bang we can conceive of.

It's a measure of our desire for something better

The more respectable face of our dark draw to destruction may be as an expression of dissatisfaction with the current state of things.

You don't have to be an all-out doomsday prepper to acknowledge the appeal. What are humans really like – what am *I* really like – when you strip back the crusty layers of modern life, the Google calendars and office politics and insurance premiums and home renos? What's really 'real' when all the trappings are gone? It's not a totally outlandish thing to wonder.

Rebecca Solnit, the writer who gave us the term 'mansplaining', probes the human experience of apocalypse-type events – from a smallpox epidemic and the London Blitz to Chernobyl, 9/11, and Hurricane Katrina – in her book *A Paradise Built in Hell: The Extraordinary Communities That Arise in Disaster*. She was struck by a strange nostalgia – her own, and other people's – for what might easily be classed as the most nightmarish days of their lives:

> When I ask people about the disasters they have lived through, I find on many faces that retrospective basking as they recount tales of Canadian ice storms, Midwestern snow days, New York City blackouts, oppressive heat in southern India, fire in New Mexico, the great earthquake in Mexico City, earlier hurricanes in Louisiana, the economic collapse in Argentina, earthquakes in California and Mexico, and a strange pleasure overall. It was the joy on their faces that surprised me ... It should not be so, is not so, in the familiar version of what disaster brings, and yet it is there, arising from rubble, from ice, from fire, from storms and floods.

What happened, for the most part, in these extreme situations was that people pulled together in ways they tend not to in peacetime and plenty. They stepped up. They improvised. They talked to their neighbours. They helped each other. They let go of petty resentments and anxieties that had seemed so important and found themselves energised by what was required of them. They discovered they were more resilient, and more needed, than they knew.

It was an experience shared to some degree by many of us in the early stages of the COVID-19 pandemic – the solidarity, the humour, the notes of unexpected grace. The rediscovery of things all but forgotten in the relentless stream of our overscheduled lives. As Solnit puts it, 'The joy matters as a measure of otherwise neglected desires, desires for public life and civil society, for inclusion, purpose, and power.'

The perverse desire to see what would happen were business as usual simply swept away may come more from a place of aspiration for a better way of doing life together than, say, a childish delight in breaking stuff.

Solnit notes that the synonyms we use for disaster have this doubleness built into them. *Emergency*, which has become a wholly negative word, first meant something that is *emerging* – a separation from the familiar, the emergence of a new atmosphere.

Catastrophe comes from a Greek term meaning *a sudden turn*: 'It means an upset of what is expected and was originally used to mean a plot twist. To emerge into the unexpected is not always terrible, though these words have evolved to imply ill fortune.'

Apocalypse, too, whether you pair it with *nuclear*, or *zombie*, or *jellyfish*, or *dating*, conjures (more efficiently than any other word we have) a future that is to be dreaded. Yet it once carried connotations of 'unveiling' or 'uncovering' rather than of wholesale destruction. First used of elements of Jewish scripture and then applied to the final book of the Christian Bible – the Apocalypse of John is now more commonly called Revelation – it does purport to tell humans about the future (the 'end of the world'), but its purpose is first and foremost to bring to light what is hidden. Reality is laid bare; justice is done. The apocalypse is to be *welcomed*.

In January 1994, a pre-dawn earthquake cut power to most of Los Angeles. The Griffith Observatory fielded phone calls from spooked locals asking about 'the strange sky'. What they were seeing was the stars.

Given that 80 percent of Europe and North America no longer experiences real darkness, the Milky Way is for many of us little more than an abstract idea, familiar from photos but not so much from real life. Solnit describes this restoration of the heavens as a feature of various disasters in recent decades, and proposes an analogy:

> You can think of the current social order as something akin to this artificial light: another kind of power that *fails* in disaster. In its place appears a reversion to improvised, collaborative, cooperative, and local society. However beautiful the stars of a suddenly visible night sky, few nowadays could find their way by them. But the constellations of solidarity, altruism, and improvisation are within most of us and reappear at these times. People know what to do in a disaster. The loss of power, the disaster in the modern sense, is an affliction, but the reappearance of these old heavens is its opposite. This is the paradise entered through hell.

We enjoy our pessimism, then; and not because we're terrible people. (Or not just because we're terrible people.) There is something deeply human about our apocaholism. At its best, it may even serve as an outlet for our frustrations with the way things are – a means of reimagining and recalibrating the direction we're headed in.

The pleasures of pessimism, however, are offset by its perils.

PART 2: THE PERILS OF PESSIMISM

I'm open to arguments that pessimism can be constructive.

I guess it's possible that a sense of impending doom can focus the mind, galvanise us into action, or at least give you something to talk about at school pick-up or with your Uber driver.

On the whole, though, I'm pessimistic about pessimism. My instinct is that it is not serving us well – and that it threatens to become a self-fulfilling prophecy.

So here are a few reasons to consider distrusting our declinism. Let's call them the four horsemen of apocaholism: error, ignorance, polarisation, and apathy.

Error: It is difficult to make predictions, especially about the future

When I lived in the UK, it rained a lot. That is to say, it rained *often*, which is not quite the same thing.

Most of the time, it starts sprinkling, you pop up the hood of your jacket, no worries. But if you're cycling around town, and you don't want to arrive at the library or at Sainsbury's with the thighs of your jeans wet through, you need to time your forays out under the lowering skies carefully.

That's where the hourly weather forecast came in. I wasn't much in the habit of checking the weather in Sydney – partly a function of driving most places, partly because, oh that's right, the sun shines a lot – but after moving to Cambridge, it became compulsive for me.

The curious thing is, the forecast was probably wrong as often as right. If it told me it would be raining at 10am, 2–4pm, and most of the evening, I'd plan my movements around the anticipated dryish spells. But there I'd be at midday, navigating the cobbled streets under a determined drizzle with a vintage wicker bike basket full of damp groceries.

Yet, no matter how many times the forecast let me down, I never stopped being surprised; and I never stopped planning my days around it. I just needed to be told *something*; and if wild guesses were all that was available, well, I'd take it.

Humans' failed predictions about the future are inexhaustible. Their number must be even greater than we think because we have a way of singling out the lone prescient voice, and at the same time letting our own miscalculations fall quietly by the wayside.

Predictions of the end of the world are no exception. The guy in a sandwich board informing the rest of us that THE END IS NIGH is a stock cultural type. Historical figures who have gone on record with a precise date for the apocalypse include Botticelli (1504), Christopher Columbus (1658), Puritan minister Cotton Mather (1697 initially, but when that didn't eventuate he revised his estimate – twice – to 1716 and then 1736), and Rasputin (2013).

When Halley's Comet returned in 1910, Earth actually passed through its tail, leading astronomer Camille Flammarion to hazard that toxic gases would 'impregnate the atmosphere and possibly snuff out all life on the planet' and spawning a hasty trade in anti-comet pills and anti-comet umbrellas. From Nostradamus to Y2K, from the Prophet Hen of Leeds (google it) to the Heaven's Gate cult, we have continually anticipated the end of the world as we know it, and – so far – thankfully – always been wrong.

Somewhere in between when it's going to rain today and when the apocalypse is due lie all the other things we're bad at predicting. In 1984, a young psychologist and political scientist called

Philip E. Tetlock was sitting in a committee meeting on US–Soviet relations and was struck by two things: that the various experts round the table were unshakably confident in their analyses; and that their forecasts flatly contradicted one another.

Over the next 20 years, Tetlock gathered more than 80,000 probability estimates about the future from 284 experts with an average of more than 12 years of experience in their particular specialty. Journalist David Epstein sums up the results:

> The experts were, by and large, horrific forecasters. Their areas of specialty, years of experience, and (for some) access to classified information made no difference. They were bad at short-term forecasting and bad at long-term forecasting. They were bad at forecasting in every domain. When experts declared that future events were impossible or nearly impossible, 15 percent of them occurred nonetheless. When they declared events to be a sure thing, more than one-quarter of them failed to transpire. As the Danish proverb warns, 'It is difficult to make predictions, especially about the future.'

Epstein notes that the more experience and credentials experts had in their field, the worse they did on average at predicting outcomes within their specialty. When events proved them wrong, instead of going back and revising their premises or methods, they had a way of doubling down –

their expertise simply made them all the more adept at fitting whatever happened (or didn't) into their pre-existing theory.

Just like me, compulsively checking my weather app, our collective desire to see into the future tends to override whatever reservations we should have about our forecasting capacities:

> Unfortunately, the world's most prominent specialists are rarely held accountable for their predictions, so we continue to rely on them even when their track records make clear that we should not. One study compiled a decade of annual dollar-to-euro exchange-rate predictions made by 22 international banks: Barclays, Citigroup, JPMorgan Chase, and others. Each year, every bank predicted the end-of-year exchange rate. The banks missed every single change of direction in the exchange rate. In six of the 10 years, the true exchange rate fell outside the *entire range* of all 22 bank forecasts.

The conclusion that – in the immortal words of British MP Michael Gove during the Brexit debate – 'people have had enough of experts' is not the only possible response to such dispiriting news. Epstein's book *Range: How Generalists Triumph in a Specialized World*, as well as Tetlock's co-authored volume *Superforecasting: The Art and Science of Prediction*, highlight practices that go some way towards mitigating our propensity for error when it comes to the future – such as working in teams, gathering information from a variety of sources, and adjusting ideas when things don't go as expected.

Still, history is full of things that seem inevitable in prospect, and ludicrous in retrospect. Conversely, it's full of things that seemed impossible in prospect and inevitable in retrospect! It is indeed difficult to make predictions, especially about the future.

This does not absolve us of our responsibility to prepare, as best we can, for tomorrow's challenges and dangers. Most of the direst forebodings of our ancestors did not come to pass; sometimes, that was because we paid attention to them and did what needed to be done. Steering between the Scylla of paralysing panic and the Charybdis of complacency (again, google it) is a task that demands constant vigilance.

Our voracious appetite for forecasting is unlikely to diminish. But in keeping with our proneness to error, it's not a bad idea to add a decent pinch of salt.

Ignorance: The prophets of progress

One side effect of the zeitgeisty pessimism of our times has been the rise of a kind of counter-movement – a rag-tag band of self-proclaimed optimists bemused (or perhaps irritated) by so many of us fretting about our culture's imminent slide into ruin.

Here's an oft-quoted gem in the optimist vs pessimist flame wars:

> Though in every age everybody knows that up to his own time progressive improvement has been taking place, nobody seems to reckon on any improvement during the next generation. We cannot absolutely prove that those are in error who say society has reached a turning point, that we have seen our best days. But so said all who came before us, and with just as much apparent reason ... On what principle is it that, when we see nothing but improvement behind us, we are to expect nothing but deterioration before us?

This is the historian Thomas Babington Macaulay, writing in 1830. Or, more pithily, here's how American humourist P. J. O'Rourke put it in the 1990s:

> In general, life is better than it ever has been, and if you think that, in the past, there was some

> golden age of pleasure and plenty to which you would, if you were able, transport yourself, let me say one single word: 'dentistry.'

In our own day, the most prominent of the prophets of progress include the Canadian psychologist Steven Pinker and Matt Ridley, a British science writer and member of the House of Lords. Pinker's interventions to help us deal with our pessimism addiction include his books *The Better Angels of Our Nature: Why Violence Has Declined* and *Enlightenment Now: The Case for Reason, Science, Humanism, and Progress.* Ridley is the author of *The Rational Optimist* and *The Evolution of Everything: How Small Changes Transform Our World.*

In November 2015, the two squared off in Toronto in front of an audience of 3000 people, as part of a Munk Debate on the topic 'Be it resolved, humankind's best days lie ahead'. Ranged against them were philosopher Alain de Botton and spotter of surprising social trends Malcolm Gladwell.

The ensuing debate entertains, as such debates tend to. It also involves these four highly educated and articulate thinkers doing a lot of talking past each other (as such debates tend to).

Pinker and Ridley insist that the data is on their side. Look back over the last 200 years, they say, or even the last 20 years. (Almost) all of the bad things are dramatically down: poverty, infant mortality, crime, disease, plane crash deaths. The good things are dramatically up: literacy, GDP, cancer survival rates, girls in school, clean water access, monitoring of endangered species. Onwards and upwards!

Their opponents do not dispute the data. But they do take issue with the tone. Though the Pinker/Ridley affirmative insist that they're *not* saying everything is either perfect or perfectible, the Gladwell/de Botton negative find them, and their statistics, a tad glib. By way of supplementing this upbeat picture, they call attention to humans' propensity to screw things up; to the epidemic levels of mental illness that in high-income countries seem to track with the kinds of improvements being talked about; and to the unprecedented nature of new threats, from climate change to global internet security.

Reading the published debate, I find myself siding with – or at least privately egging on – the negative. I can't disagree with Pinker and Ridley that child mortality dropping by two-thirds in the last 50 years, or deaths from malaria decreasing by 60 percent in the last 15 years, or oil spills being down by 90 percent since the 1970s make the world a better place. Children not dying is better than children dying! And the counterargument that high-income countries and high-income people have plenty of problems of their own hardly gainsays the fact that it is better to be healthy and to have enough to eat than not. That, given a choice between which problems you could have, you would choose Switzerland's over Sudan's any day.

And yet, my heart is against them. Something about their breezy optimism rankles.

Someone whose approach helped steer me out of this impasse was a Swedish doctor and public health specialist called Hans Rosling. Rosling worked in India and Mozambique, discovered a previously unrecognised paralytic disease, founded Médecins Sans Frontières in Sweden, was an adviser to the World Health Organization and UNICEF, and in 2014 dropped everything to be on the ground in Liberia helping to curb the Ebola epidemic. He was not exactly your average armchair optimist.

In fact, Rosling doesn't fit all that neatly into the optimist/pessimist divide. He draws on much of the data beloved of the prophets of progress, but carefully avoids being boosterish or polemical. In his book *Factfulness: Ten Reasons We're Wrong About the World – and Why Things Are Better Than You Think*, published after his death in 2017, Rosling explains:

> People often call me an optimist, because I show them the enormous progress they didn't know about. That makes me angry. I'm not an optimist. That makes me sound naïve. I'm a very serious 'possibilist.' That's something I made up. It means someone who neither hopes without reason, nor fears without reason … I see no conflict between celebrating this progress and continuing to fight for more.
>
> … It seems that when we hear someone say things are getting better, we think they are also saying 'don't worry, relax' or even 'look away.' But when I say things are getting better, I am not saying those things at all … I am saying that things can be both bad and better.

For decades, as Rosling travelled the world speaking to politicians and aid organisations, to scientists and activists, to multinationals, universities, the World Economic Forum and the African Union and the UN, he would have his audiences complete a simple quiz about the state of the world: what percentage of girls across the world finish primary school? What is current global life expectancy? How many people die as a result of natural disasters? How many people have electricity?

No matter where he went, people did badly on the quiz. Very badly. Worse, in fact, than they probably would have had they just randomly selected answers without looking at the questions.

Even the people most closely involved in dealing with the world's biggest problems believed that things were much worse than they are.

Did you know that around a billion people have moved out of extreme poverty in the last couple of decades?

Did you know that 80 percent of one-year-old children worldwide have received some vaccination – that almost everyone goes to school – that the global population is expected to level out by the end of this century?

Did you know that our collective efforts to do something about hunger and disease and child mortality have been *working*?

You can do the Factfulness quiz online, or in Rosling's book. (Most people fail – though now I've given you some spoilers, I have every confidence you will ace it.) Its goal is not to imply that everything is just fine actually, you can all stop feeling guilty about the state of the world and get on with your lives. The danger of our relative ignorance about how things used to be, and how many things are improving, is not only that we will feel more anxious about the present and future than may be warranted. It's also that we may give up on doing things that are in fact working, or in desperation adopt more drastic and less effective measures.

The benefits of what Hans Rosling christens 'factfulness' are reflected in the world of fundraising. Gone, for the most part, from the way aid agencies run their campaigns are the heart-rending images of malnourished children from the TV ads and billboards and Band Aid albums of the 1980s and 90s. In polls by Oxfam and others, many people report that such negative portrayals seem to them 'depressing, manipulative, and hopeless', and make them feel like conditions in the poorest countries will never improve.

By contrast, try following the child sponsorship organisation Compassion on Instagram. The ear-to-ear smiles, inspirational stories, and videos of kids meeting their sponsors for the first time represent more than the upbeat curatorial pressures of social media. Celebration and compassion should go hand in hand.

Whether your nightmare future scenario is related to poverty or climate change, race relations or educational standards, a constructive response will build in an understanding of where we've come from. Just as a growing body of research emphasises the practice of gratitude as a potent antidote to anxiety on an individual psychological level, the celebration of wins – large and small – could go some way to tempering our collective pessimism. A 'factful' approach to the past and the present helps us honour those who've fought hard for change, and motivate others to get involved.

Polarisation: Our greatest safety

The enigmatic writer David Foster Wallace famously tells the story of two young fish swimming along one day when they pass an older fish, who says, 'Morning, boys, how's the water?' Swimming on, eventually one of them turns to the other and says, 'What the hell is water?'

My 'how's the water' moment – the point at which the pessimism we're all swimming in suddenly became visible to me – came when I read these words from the Pulitzer Prize-winning novelist and essayist Marilynne Robinson:

> Cultural pessimism is always fashionable, and, since we are human, there are always grounds for it. It has the negative consequence of depressing the level of aspiration, the sense of the possible. And from time to time it has the extremely negative consequence of encouraging a kind of somber panic, a collective dream-state in which recourse to terrible remedies is inspired by delusions of mortal threat. If there is anything

> in the life of any culture or period that gives good grounds for alarm, it is the rise of cultural pessimism, whose major passion is bitter hostility toward many or most of the people within the very culture the pessimists always feel they are intent on rescuing.

Pessimism is perennially 'in', as noted already. Yet I want to suggest that one of the forces amplifying it in our own time is a growing partisanship.

It's not simply that everything's going to hell in a handcart; *they* are the ones driving it there. Whoever 'they' are, part of the pleasure we take in our pessimism lies in our outrage, our self-righteousness – the conviction that a significant portion of our fellow citizens are dangerous lunatics, or at least up that end of the political spectrum, and that they're ruining everything.

Do a quick mental exercise here: think of an issue on which you deeply believe yourself to be in the right, and the views of those who disagree with you to be not only mistaken but harmful. Imagine your opponents got their way and had their policy put in place. If it turned out not to have the disastrous effects you feared – if it even made things better, by the measure you were using – would you be relieved to be wrong?

In other words, which do I (honestly) value more: the common good, or my side being right?

One symptom of this polarisation is to be found in the disconnect between people's optimism about their own situation and their pessimism about the bigger picture.

Take the current epicentre of partisan politics, the United States. Back in 2016, as the presidential primaries kicked off, an Aspen Institute poll found that, while only 36 percent of Americans thought their country as a whole was headed in the right direction, 85 percent said they were very or somewhat satisfied with their own position in life and ability to pursue the American dream.

As the journalist James Fallows asks, reasonably enough: 'What explains the gulf between most American's hopeful outlook on areas and institutions they know directly and their despair about the country they know only through the news?'

And that gap is by no means a uniquely American phenomenon. A UK poll asked people in different areas how big a problem they felt things like immigration, teen pregnancy, unemployment, crime, and drugs were, both in their local area and in the country as a whole. Predictably enough, people consistently rated the problems as more significant *out there* than *round here.*

This kind of 'two-track thinking' was also present

in the interviews with Australian youth referenced earlier for their apocalyptic eagerness. Researchers noted that many young people continued to be optimistic about their personal futures while expecting disaster on a macro-global scale. Their plans to (for example) get that commerce degree and a decent Instagram following and an eventual mortgage and 2.3 kids were curiously insulated from the imminent collapse of society.

Of course, it's natural for young people to have a certain buoyancy about their future; and it's natural for us to think that the world in general is a scarier place than where I live – almost regardless of where it is I live. As Hans Rosling puts it, rather sweetly, '"out there" is the sum of millions of places, while you live in just one place. Of course more bad things happen out there: out there is much bigger than here.'

But when it comes to our sense of national trends in particular, this skewing effect is often deliberately cultivated, and not benign. Fear as a political tool is powerful but not easily controlled. One trope that was invoked in US politics in 2016 was the idea of a 'Flight 93 election'. Flight 93, you may recall, was the United Airlines flight that on September 11, 2001, crashed into a field in Pennsylvania as passengers and crew attempted to retake control of the plane from four al-Qaeda terrorists.

By analogy, a 'Flight 93' election is one where 'you charge the cockpit or you die' – and you may well die anyway. Once this grim outlook governs the way we approach democratic elections – it's do or die, our side or the end of the world – it seems fair to say that pessimism itself has become a problem.

Robinson, dissecting our cultural pessimism, continues:

> When panic on one side is creating alarm on the other, it is easy to forget that there are always as good grounds for optimism as for pessimism – exactly the same grounds, in fact – that is, because we are human. We still have every potential for good we have ever had, and the same presumptive claim to respect, our own respect and one another's. We are still creatures of singular interest and value, agile of soul as we have always been and as we will continue to be even despite our errors and depredations, for as long as we abide on this earth. To value one another is our greatest safety, and to indulge in fear and contempt is our gravest error.

There's an important anthropological element here. Paradoxically, one of our culture's less helpful contributions to the way we all relate to each other is the baseline presumption that humans are basically good. Though it *sounds* hopeful and kind, in practice it produces a harshness that undermines our best efforts to build a stable, functional polity.

Our democracies were founded on what is, on the face of it, a far more pessimistic understanding of human nature. The key revolutions of the modern era – the French, the Russian – took a rosier view of the perfectibility of humans: with the right education, with the right political system, everything would fall into place. Our messy democracies, on the other hand, were premised on the idea that nothing can be perfected, and none of us can be trusted.

That premise was an explicitly Christian one. The doctrine of original sin – the seemingly harsh judgment that we are both corrupt, and shockingly corruptible – necessitated a system of checks and balances, a system that did not allow too much power to any one individual or institution. Strangely, it is the affirmation of the darkness and incorrigible self-deception of our hearts that gives us the wriggle room to give one another the wriggle room to fail, and to build. A sunny optimism about human nature has a way of making us cynical, and our social systems brittle and volatile.

The British writer Francis Spufford explains

that such an optimism fails to map onto reality as we actually experience it:

> Our destructiveness is a truth about us just as basic as our capacity for love … If you accept this, the refusal to admit it in contemporary culture starts to look silly, and worse than silly. It locks us collectively into a cycle of indulgence and surprise. Most of the time, there's the fingers-in-ears denial that anything could ever be wrong, periodically interrupted by stagy astonishment when something goes so wrong it can't be ignored … In comparison, Christianity says that both less and more is to be expected of people. Less because of our inevitably divided and thwarting selves; more because thanks to grace our identities are more provisional, more hopefully fluid, than we commonly acknowledge.

As Robinson notes, our humanity ceaselessly offers us grounds both for pessimism and for optimism. Members of a pluralist democracy stand in need of both: a healthy pessimism, one that begins with me rather than my opponent, with an acknowledgment that *I* am the problem; and an optimism that includes the other – that imagines and hopes on their behalf, that chooses recognition over incomprehension.

Our cultural pessimism is itself becoming a greater threat than many of the crises it feeds on. Once we stop recognising ourselves as bound together in a common future, we lose much of the power we have to shape that future. *To value one another is our greatest safety, and to indulge in fear and contempt is our gravest error.*

Apathy: All the running you can do

There is a moment in Lewis Carroll's *Through the Looking Glass* – the even trippier sequel to *Alice's Adventures in Wonderland* – when suddenly, mid-conversation, Alice and the Red Queen begin to run.

'Faster! Faster!' the Queen cries. Yet they never seem to pass anything, and end up under the same tree they started at.

'In *our* country,' Alice says, 'you'd generally get to somewhere else – if you ran very fast for a long time, as we've been doing.'

'A slow sort of country!' exclaims the Queen. 'Now, *here*, you see, it takes all the running *you* can do, to keep in the same place. If you want to get somewhere else, you must run at least twice as fast as that!'

One of the great frustrations of modern political life (of human life in general?) is that nothing is ever finally settled. Each issue, policy, system, or belief must be re-established, re-argued, fought for over again in every generation, or even each election cycle. Though we may want to lock things down – to secure particular rights or make particular gains in progress, and then tick that box and move on to something else – achievements of any kind have a pesky way of not staying put.

You don't get to cultivate a free press and then freeze it in place forever; you don't get to build a functional health care system and then cross that off your communal to-do list. As it turns out, you don't get to assume that we've sorted once and for all, and to the satisfaction of every citizen, questions like the preferability of democracy to autocracy, or the efficacy of vaccines.

It's like the second law of thermodynamics but for societies: the natural tendency of a system, without constant input, will be to degenerate into a disordered state. Most of the time, it takes all the running we can do simply to keep the current state of things from collapsing in a heap.

This dispiriting reality has perhaps never been articulated more unflinchingly than in the ancient Jewish book of wisdom called Ecclesiastes. 'I have seen all the things that are done under the sun', writes the 'Teacher', held by rabbinic and Christian tradition to be King Solomon. 'All of them are meaningless, a chasing after the wind.'

What do people gain from all their labours
  at which they toil under the sun?
Generations come and generations go,
  but the earth remains for ever.
The sun rises and the sun sets,
  and hurries back to where it rises.
The wind blows to the south
  and turns to the north;
round and round it goes,
  ever returning on its course.
All streams flow into the sea,
  yet the sea is never full.
To the place the streams come from,
  there they return again.
All things are wearisome,
  more than one can say.
The eye never has enough of seeing,
  nor the ear its fill of hearing.
What has been will be again,
  what has been done will be done again;
  there is nothing new under the sun.
Is there anything of which one can say,
  'Look! This is something new'?
It was here already, long ago;
  it was here before our time.
No one remembers the former generations,
  and even those yet to come
will not be remembered
  by those who follow them.

(Ecclesiastes 1:14; 1:3–11)

This is life 'under the sun'. This is history repeating itself. This is weary pessimism in the face of the ceaseless stream of time, in the face of a future that demands the same efforts of us, over and over and over again.

The Teacher gives voice to this apathy right up front – these are some of the opening words of the book. But if this could be described as the glass-half-empty vision of entropic human life, the glass-half-full version of the same relentless, cyclical reality comes not long afterwards:

> There is a time for everything,
>   and a season for every activity under the heavens:
> a time to be born and a time to die,
> a time to plant and a time to uproot,
> a time to kill and a time to heal,
> a time to tear down and a time to build,
> a time to weep and a time to laugh,
> a time to mourn and a time to dance,
> a time to scatter stones and a time to gather them,
> a time to embrace and a time to refrain from
>   embracing,
> a time to search and a time to give up,
> a time to keep and a time to throw away,
> a time to tear and a time to mend,
> a time to be silent and a time to speak,
> a time to love and a time to hate,
> a time for war and a time for peace.
>
> (Ecclesiastes 3:1–8)

In place of cynicism or despair, the Teacher advocates an acceptance of the need to discern what this particular moment requires, and to gear up for that. Again.

He goes on:

> What do workers gain from their toil? I have seen the burden God has laid on the human race. He has made everything beautiful in its time. He has also set eternity in the human heart; yet no one can fathom what God has done from beginning to end. I know that there is nothing better for people than to be happy and to do good while they live. That each of them may eat and drink, and find satisfaction in all their toil – this is the gift of God.
>
> (Ecclesiastes 3:9–13)

There is no autopilot, for individuals or for societies. There is ever the longing for perfection, for permanence – *he has set eternity in the human heart* – and there is the reality of limitation, the good that I can do while I live, in the particular crisis of this moment.

What is required, then – and what an enervating pessimism makes all the more difficult – is the constant renewal of energies for tasks that must be performed fresh in each generation, and repeatedly within each generation. Which means that what is required is the resistance of apathy, and the constant renewal of patience, and of hope.

CONCLUSION: STATEMENTS OF FAITH

In the depths of World War II, John Steinbeck wrote to a friend:

> All the goodness and the heroisms will rise up again, then be cut down again and rise up. It isn't that the evil thing wins – it never will – but that it doesn't die.

This sounds nice. And coming from the pen of one of the great American novelists, the weight of the rhetoric reinforces our intuitive sense that he's telling us something true about life.

In fact, like almost everything we believe most deeply about the world we live in, this is a statement of faith. Steinbeck can prove neither that the evil thing will never win, nor that it won't die. Our optimism or pessimism (or both) about the future are at core a function of what it is we believe about human nature, and the bedrock nature of reality itself.

Once you notice that, these statements of faith show up everywhere. Sometimes they're consciously speculative; sometimes they carry an air of simply stating self-evident truths.

Here's a few more.

First, this reflection from Mark Manson, one of the prophets of doom currently to be found on airport bookshelves throughout the land, in his book *Everything Is F*cked*:

> If I worked at Starbucks, instead of writing people's names on their coffee cup, I'd write the following:
>
> *One day, you and everyone you love will die. And beyond a small group of people for an extremely brief period of time, little of what you say or do will ever matter. This is the Uncomfortable Truth of Life. And everything you think or do is but an elaborate avoidance of it. We are inconsequential cosmic dust, bumping and milling about on a tiny blue speck. We imagine our own importance. We invent our purpose – we are nothing.*
>
> *Enjoy your ... coffee.*

For Manson, hope – and meaning, and purpose – are a mere trick that we humans play on ourselves to get through the day.

Another option might be the idiosyncratic mix of optimism and pessimism articulated by the philosopher Alain de Botton – pessimism about human nature, but optimism for a future that doesn't include us:

> I'm optimistic for a species that is not *Homo sapiens*. I believe that it is possible that maybe in a thousand years' time we will create a species that doesn't die, which is properly able to use knowledge, and is happy, and inherently non-aggressive. But it won't be *Homo sapiens*; it will be another species. I could be optimistic but just not on behalf of humanity. There's a better-designed *Homo* that might be coming some point in five hundred years. It's not us.

By way of contrast, here's Theodore Parker, a nineteenth-century minister and abolitionist, holding forth in an 1853 sermon on the topic of 'Justice and the Conscience':

> I do not pretend to understand the moral universe, the arc is a long one, my eye reaches but little ways. I cannot calculate the curve and complete the figure by the experience of sight; I can divine it by conscience. But from what I see I am sure it bends towards justice.

Parker's image of a moral arc was popularised by Martin Luther King Jr, and his conviction about the moral fabric of the universe inspired and sustained the non-violent resistance of the civil rights movement. These underlying assumptions about where everything is headed powerfully shape our choices, and especially our pursuit of justice.

Or take William Wilberforce, whose 20-year struggle against the transatlantic slave trade was also a struggle against the fear and pessimism of his contemporaries. While they saw only economic ruin and social upheaval in his proposals, he was convinced that, whatever the evidence suggested, what was morally right would also prove beneficial overall.

In a celebrated speech to the British parliament in 1789, Wilberforce countered the 'sensible' concerns of his fellow MPs:

> It naturally suggested itself to me, how strange it was that Providence, however mysterious in its ways, should so have constituted the world, as to make one part of it depend for its existence on the depopulation and devastation of another.
>
> I could not, therefore, help distrusting the arguments of those who insisted that the plundering of Africa was necessary for the cultivation of the West Indies. I could not believe that the same Being, who forbids rapine and bloodshed, had made rapine and bloodshed necessary to the well-being of any part of his universe …
>
> I wish to observe, with submission, but with perfect conviction of heart, what an instance is this, how safely we may trust the rules of justice, the dictates of conscience, and the laws of God, in opposition even to the seeming impolicy of these eternal principles.

For my part, I believe – with Parker and King and Wilberforce – that the world is so constituted that virtue and flourishing are closely connected.

I believe that hope is not something I need to trick myself into, but the deep logic of the universe in which we live.

I believe, with Steinbeck, that the evil thing will never win; and, contra Steinbeck, I believe that the evil thing will one day die. I believe that there will be a true 'apocalypse': a laying bare of reality, an ultimate justice, a liberation from the cycles of history and the faultiness of *Homo sapiens* that doesn't involve passing the baton to a superior race and going gently into the good night. An apocalypse which culminates in the death of death itself, when God will wipe every tear from the eyes of his people. That apocalypse will indeed be welcome.

Until that day, I believe that, in the economy of the Creator, we don't have to choose between doing the things that bring people out of poverty *and* the things that shore up human freedom *and* the things that conserve and renew the earth *and* the things that lead to strong communities.

This is not to say that everything will be just fine. History reminds us that lots of things could go very badly, and some no doubt will. But a humble pessimism about human nature, coupled with a grounded hopefulness about the world, will be our friend as we process and respond to the manifold challenges of our particular moment.

The hows, of course, are the difficulty. John W. Gardner, an adviser to several US presidents, used to say that what we face are breathtaking opportunities disguised as insoluble problems.

To sign off, then, a blessing upon you: may you have the pessimism to look steadily and unflinchingly at the problems, and the optimism to perceive and pursue the opportunities hiding behind them.

NOTES

These references are not exhaustive, but mostly intended to point you in the right direction if there's something you want to track down or dig into a bit further.

INTRODUCTION: WELCOME TO THE APOCALYPSE

Page 2: the jellification of the oceans. I first read about the 'jellyfish apocalypse' in Tim Flannery's superb article in *The New York Review of Books* on Lisa-ann Gershwin's book *Stung: On Jellyfish Blooms and the Future of the Ocean.* It's called 'They're Taking Over!' and was published in September 2013. But, look, I'm no expert on marine life, and (like just about every other apocalyptic prediction) the data's disputed. Try pairing Flannery (or Gershwin's book) with 'Are swarms of jellyfish taking over the ocean?', an article by Martha Henriques published on the BBC Earth site in September 2016.

Cassandra vs Chicken Little

Page 6: the menu of apocalyptic snacks and side dishes. Almost all of these are real-life headlines, or slight variations on them. *Weapons of Math Destruction: How Big Data Increases Inequality and Threatens Democracy* is a book by Cathy O'Neil (we read it in my book club last year). Also, 'The Really Big One' by Kathryn Schulz, published in The New Yorker in July 2015, is well worth one of your monthly quota of free articles. If you're a subscriber, hey, read it every month. It's excellent.

Page 11: 'More than at any time in history'. The Woody Allen piece is called 'My Speech to the Graduates', and you can read a digitised version on the *New York Times* website.

PART I: THE PLEASURES OF PESSIMISM

Page 13: The stories of Johnny O and the Earls are both from the first episode of Season 2 of *Doomsday Preppers*, 'You Can't Let Evil Win' (which, truth be told, is the only episode I watched). For the record, I know Johnny says here that preppers are the ones you'll turn to when the nuclear waste hits the fan, but can I advise you not to go to Johnny's house at that point? That preparedness drill he was running for his family wasn't about defending his home against terrorists – he has a bunch of guns on hand to use on the hapless masses fleeing disaster who might want to steal his food or, I don't know, massacre his family. STEER CLEAR.

Page 15: 'The blog Calculated Risk is always a reliable turn-on'. Hugo Lindgren, 'Pessimism Porn', *New York Magazine*, 30 January 2009.

Page 16: 'It's easy, for me anyway'. For the surveys of Australian youth, see Julia Cook, '"How Much Do I Want the Apocalypse to Happen and Just Wipe This All Clean?": The Use of Apocalyptic Narratives by

Non-religious Youth', *Journal for the Academic Study of Religion* 30.1 (2017): 52–72.

It's in

Page 17: 'I know that it is thought essential'. The Mill quote is from a 'Speech on Perfectibility' he delivered in 1828.

It's thrilling

Page 19: 'wartime delight in annihilation'. See Lowe's chapter 'The End of the World' for all the quotations in this section.

It's a measure of our desire for something better

Page 21: 'When I ask people about the disasters'. See Solnit's 'Prelude: Falling Together', pp. 6 and 10, for the quotations used here. I also drew on Amanda Petrusich's article 'Fear of the light: why we need darkness', published in *The Guardian* on 23 August 2016, for the stuff on light pollution and the 1994 Los Angeles earthquake.

PART 2: THE PERILS OF PESSIMISM

Error: It is difficult to make predictions, especially about the future

Page 26: I just needed to be told something. Even though I rarely checked the weather pre-UK, I've kept the habit since returning to sunny Sydney. My current weather app is actually not that much more reliable than what I was using over there, but my irrational and compulsive dependence on it shows no signs of flagging.

Page 28: 'The experts were, by and large', 'Unfortunately, the world's most prominent specialists'. David Epstein's article 'The Peculiar Blindness of Experts' can be found in the June 2019 issue of *The Atlantic.*

Page 30: the Scylla of paralysing panic and the Charybdis of complacency. It's, like, a classical reference. Odysseus had to navigate between the six-headed monster Scylla and the whirlpool Charybdis, stationed on either side of a narrow channel. His encounters with these sea monsters weren't super-successful, actually, but he did survive.

Ignorance: The prophets of progress

Page 31: 'Though in every age everybody knows'. Macaulay's gem comes from an essay of 1830 written in disagreement with the perceived pessimism of Robert Southey, the English Poet Laureate at the time.

Page 31: 'In general, life is better than it ever has been'. You can find the P. J. O'Rourke quotation in the opening pages of his book, the unsqueamishly titled *All the Trouble in the World: The Lighter Side of Overpopulation, Famine, Ecological Disaster, Ethnic Hatred, Plague, and Poverty* (1994).

Page 32: In November 2015, the two squared off. You can read the Munk Debate in full (along with pre-debate interviews with the four participants) in an attractive little volume called *Do Humankind's Best Days Lie Ahead?*

Page 35: 'People often call me an optimist'. Rosling's

explanation that he thinks of himself as a 'possibilist' appears in Chapter Two of his book, titled 'The Negativity Instinct'. In Chapter 10 of *Factfulness*, 'The Urgency Instinct', Rosling outlines the five global risks he says we should worry about: 'global pandemic, financial collapse, world war, climate change, and extreme poverty. Why is it that these problems cause me most concern? Because they are quite likely to happen: the first three have all happened before and the other two are happening now; and because each has the potential to cause mass suffering either directly or indirectly by pausing human progress for many years or decades. If we fail here, nothing else will work. These are mega killers that we must avoid, if at all possible, by acting collaboratively and step-by-step.' Writing these words in coronavirus lockdown, I'm more convinced than ever that this guy knew what he was talking about.

Page 37: In polls by Oxfam and others. You can read the December 2012 press release from Oxfam in full on their website under the heading 'Show Africa's potential not just its problems, says Oxfam'.

Polarisation: Our greatest safety

Page 38: 'What the hell is water?' The fish-in-water story comes from a commencement speech David Foster Wallace gave at Kenyon College, Ohio, which was published in *The Guardian* in September 2008, just after his death.

Page 38: 'Cultural pessimism is always fashionable'. Marilynne Robinson's remarks here (and below, p. 42) come towards the end of her essay 'Reformation' in *The Givenness of Things* (2015).

Page 40: Back in 2016. James Fallows dissects the gap between the local and national American experience in his May 2018 *Atlantic* article 'The Reinvention of America'.

Page 40: A UK poll asked people. These survey results come from a 2013 Ipsos MORI report, which can be found in graph form (along with a lot of other fascinating material) at ourworldindata.org/optimism-pessimism.

Page 40: This kind of 'two-track thinking'. For the personal optimism of young Australians, see Julia Cook, 'Young adults' hopes for the long-term future: from re-enchantment with technology to faith in humanity', *Journal of Youth Studies* 19.4 (2016): 517–532. She references the idea of 'two-track thinking' from a 2010 paper, 'Stumbling towards collapse: coming to terms with the climate crisis', by Terry Leahy, Vanessa Bowden, and Steven Threadgold, in *Environmental Politics* 19.9: 851–868.

Page 41: "'out there' is the sum of millions of places'. Hans Rosling makes this observation about how dangerous things are 'out there' in Chapter 5 of his *Factfulness* book, 'The Size Instinct'.

Page 44: 'Our destructiveness is a truth about us'. This comes from Spufford's delightful (and delightfully titled) 2012 book *Unapologetic: Why, Despite Everything, Christianity Can Still Make Surprising Emotional Sense*, Chapter 8, 'Consequences'.

Apathy: All the running you can do

Page 46: Ecclesiastes 1:14; 1:3–11. If you're new to it, here's how Bible references work: the name of the book is followed by the chapter number and verse(s) - so here, the book of Ecclesiastes, chapter 1, verse 14, then jumping back to verses 3 to 11. The translation I'm using is the New International Version - Anglicised (2011) (NIVUK).

CONCLUSION: STATEMENTS OF FAITH

Page 51: 'All the goodness and the heroisms'. This quotation comes from a letter Steinbeck wrote on 1 January 1941 to his friend Pascal Covici. I read about it in Maria Popova's Brain Pickings blog in an entry titled 'John Steinbeck on Good and Evil, the Necessary Contradictions of the Human Nature, and Our Grounds for Lucid Hope'.

Page 52: 'If I worked at Starbucks'. The first chapter of Manson's book *Everything Is F*cked: A Book About Hope* is called 'The Uncomfortable Truth', and the Starbucks bit is in that. If you're thinking 'mate, there's no way you could actually manage to write all that on a coffee cup, even the venti or trenta options', here's what he says next: 'I'd have to write it in really tiny lettering, of course. And it'd take a while to write, meaning the line of morning rush-hour customers would be backed out the door. Not exactly stellar customer service, either. This is probably just one of the reasons I'm not employable.'

Page 53: 'I'm optimistic for a species that is not Homo

sapiens'. You can find Alain de Botton's sweeping impulse to write off our species altogether expressed in his pre-debate interview with Rudyard Griffiths, the chair of the Munk Debate, in *Do Humankind's Best Days Lie Ahead?*

Page 54: 'It naturally suggested itself to me'. The text of Wilberforce's address to the House of Lords on 12 May 1789 is widely available online.

Page 56: 'breathtaking opportunities disguised as insoluble problems. I had some issues with this quotation (hence the paraphrasing). I first heard it cited as a Franklin D. Roosevelt cusp-of-WWII thing. But the internet seems a bit more confident that this John W. Gardner guy said it. I've seen other names linked to some version of it too. If you feel like heading down that rabbit hole, well, God speed you on your way, and let me know what you find.

www.ingramcontent.com/pod-product-compliance
Lightning Source LLC
Chambersburg PA
CBHW060037050426
42448CB00012B/3058

* 9 7 8 0 6 4 7 5 3 0 7 5 7 *